Y0-AWG-367

THE SECRET KINGDOM
LEADER'S GUIDE

THE SECRET KINGDOM
LEADER'S GUIDE

PAT ROBERTSON
with BOB SLOSSER

prepared by
LESLIE H. STOBBE

THOMAS NELSON PUBLISHERS
Nashville • Camden • New York

Copyright © 1983 Pat Robertson, Bob Slosser, Leslie Stobbe

All rights reserved. Written permission must be secured from the publisher to use or reproduce any part of this book, except for brief quotations in critical reviews or articles.

Published in Nashville, Tennessee, by Thomas Nelson, Inc. and distributed in Canada by Lawson Falle, Ltd., Cambridge, Ontario.

All Scripture quotations are taken from the New American Standard Bible, © The Lockman Foundation 1960, 1962, 1963, 1968, 1971, 1972, 1973, 1975 and are used by permission.

ISBN 0-8407-5877-4

CONTENTS

CONTENTS

The Approach

Jesus said, "If any man is willing to do His will, he shall know of the teaching, whether it is of God, or whether I speak from Myself" (John 7:17). With those words He set the standard by which to test solution-oriented teaching. This leader's guide is designed to help your group begin to *do* the teaching in *The Secret Kingdom.* That's why you'll find the material oriented to interactive discussion, with you serving more as a facilitator than a teacher.

Many of the lessons call for advance preparation. That's why you will find it helpful to scan the entire book for materials to prepare in advance. Make a list of those activities that call for a variety of materials to be gleaned from magazines and newspapers, since this will alert you to potentially helpful materials weeks before you actually use them.

One of the keys to turning these truths into life-changing experiences is to insist rather strongly that students complete the lessons in advance of the class session. Not only will they participate more actively, but they will already be able to share personal experiences from implementation of the laws of the kingdom. Only as the students realize this is not an information-dispensing class but a life-involvement session will they take the student response material seriously.

If your class has never broken up into small groups, you may experience resistance to this approach. Yet you will find that a five- to eight-minute interaction in a group of three or four on a Bible passage has amazingly positive results. Whatever a learner discovers in those sessions and is forced to share with someone has a way of becoming a permanent feature of the memory bank.

Finally, remember that the atmosphere in the room is most important to the learning/doing process. Group members should preferably be facing each other in a square or circle. If you use an overhead projector, have all the sheets ready for instant use. You can lose the attention of the group quickly if you are not ready to move when they are or if there is frequent traffic in and out of the room. For that reason children should not be part of a study group of this kind.

Above all, seek the guidance of the Holy Spirit as you approach the preparation of each lesson. You cannot change people, but He can! Under His guidance the truths in these lessons can turn the world upside down in your "corner."

THE SECRET KINGDOM
LEADER'S GUIDE

THE TWO WORLDS

Key Scripture: Matt. 24:4–12

Objectives

1. To understand the significance of the crises in the visible world.
2. To learn how the visible world is interpenetrated by an invisible world established by Jesus.
3. To begin to act in faith that the invisible world's power is available to us.

Leader Preparation

1. Read chapters one and two in *The Secret Kingdom.*
2. Reread the Bible passages in the footnotes, underlining any words that speak of or point to the visible world in contrast to the invisible world.

3. Cut out newspaper headlines that refer to the problems being experienced in the visible world economically, politically, morally, spiritually.
4. Similarly cut out or highlight headlines pointing to Jesus' activity in the invisible world today. You are more likely to find these in religious magazines and newspapers.
5. Ask two or more who are experiencing real problems in the visible world to prepare short statements highlighting their difficulties. Alternatively, ask a panel consisting of a business person, a professional person like a lawyer or family counselor, and a parent of younger children to discuss key issues in the crisis facing us.
6. Work through the student material, highlighting questions that lend themselves to interaction in the group.

Setting the Stage

1. If you have a small group and a good number of headlines, place one on each seat before the group arrives. Once the group has settled in, ask each person to read the headline on his seat. Move into opening prayer and have a group member focus on several of the situations in prayer.
2. Alternatively, after prayer introduce those who will highlight difficulties in the visible world, either by personal statement or through the panel discussion (limit this to ten minutes). The objective is to bring some of the national trends into local focus.
3. Ask: "Is Jesus surprised this is happening in the world today?" Read Matthew 24:4–12 to back up answers given.

Facing the Issues

If you have group members able to discuss each of the five issues, alert them during the week to be prepared for a two-minute presentation on one of the five issue-oriented questions. If you do not have such persons, ask members of the group to give their answers from the study guide.

Facing the New Reality

1. For question two (*Facing the New Reality* in the Study Guide), have the group divide into networks of two to three people so they can discuss the experience of Elisha and his servant. You may want to give each group a slip of paper with the following questions on it: What was the reality in the scene, according to the servant? How did Elisha draw on the invisible reality? What made the difference in attitude between the servant and Elisha? What was the invisible reality in Elisha's world? Time limit: five minutes.
2. In focusing on the experience of the disciples in the boat with Jesus, you may want to ask: What were the disciples focusing on when they became afraid? Whose presence should have guaranteed safety? Why does the presence of Jesus in our life not guarantee confidence in the face of the danger? What alone can help us overcome fear of the events in the visible world?

Making It Happen

Give the group members time to record their personal involvement in the invisible kingdom. Then ask one or two to share what they recorded. Be sure the group understands this is to be an act of faith in the face of fear.

15

SESSION TWO
ENTERING THE KINGDOM

Key Scripture: John 3:1–16; Eph. 2:4–7; 1 Cor. 2:12–13

Objectives

1. To understand how we enter the secret kingdom through the new birth.
2. To grasp the truth that we have access to the abundance of God as participants in the secret kingdom.
3. To begin to experience the abundance of the kingdom by "speaking out" what God communicates to us in our communion with Him.

Leader Preparation

1. Read chapters three and four of *The Secret Kingdom*.
2. Read the Scripture passages footnoted at the bottom of the

page out of their context in the chapter. Then take a sheet of paper, write Chapter Three at the top, and list the subheads under that. Leave enough space between subheads to write in the Scripture references for that section. Now do the same for Chapter Four. Repeat, reading all the Scripture passages. This will help you focus the biblical ideas in your mind to make it possible for the Holy Spirit to "bring to your remembrance all that I said to you" (John 14:26) as you lead the discussion.

3. The Bible has a lot to say about a positive mindset. Look up the word "mind" in a Bible concordance. Make a list of the negative things emanating from the mind, as well as positive statements about our mind and our attitudes. If you have an overhead transparency, transfer the information onto a two-column chart.

4. Make a list of those in your class who have not yet entered the invisible kingdom of God. Pray specifically for each one's salvation every day of this week. Be prepared to invite them to accept Christ as personal Savior at the end of the group discussion. One of the booklets used in one-on-one witnessing, such as *The Four Spiritual Laws,* can help you be more relaxed. Your Christian bookstore will be happy to show you samples.

5. Call two class members and ask them to be ready to recreate the scene between Jesus and Nicodemus. Even if they only read the conversation seated facing each other, it will make the scene more real. A few stage props will add greatly to the impact. We too often read this very dramatic incident without catching any of the emotion.

Setting the Stage

Dan was a deeply concerned husband and father. Though his wages covered rent and food, there was little left over. He knew that his preschool son needed a new outfit, his daughter badly needed a new coat, his wife had not had a new dress in nearly two years, and his only dress suit was threadbare. Then he read that if you want

God to answer prayer, you need to be specific. Kneeling in prayer he spread the family's needs before the Lord, naming each item.

One month later Dan and his wife were asked by their pastor, "Would you folks mind if another family helped you this Christmas?" Since he had not shared his concerns with even his wife, Dan was dumbfounded, but managed to say, "Oh no, not at all. We are not too proud to accept help."

Ten days later two women, a mother and daughter, took Dan's wife and children shopping as their expression of love to Jesus at Christmas. When they returned, every member of the family had received exactly what Dan had voiced in prayer, plus numerous other items of clothing. His wife received a gift certificate that covered the purchase of a five-piece outfit for herself and a new suit for Dan.

Is Dan's experience one of those rare manifestations of answered prayer that are available only to special saints? Or is Dan's experience an example of what is available to all who live in the abundance of the invisible kingdom? After asking these questions, suggest that today's study will show how to see, enter, and enjoy the abundance of the invisible kingdom.

Entering the New Reality

1. Call upon the two you have asked to represent Jesus and Nicodemus to dramatically present the scene in John 3:1–16. Alternatively, divide the class into two groups and have them read responsively only the words of Jesus and Nicodemus.

2. Ask: "What new reality do we enter when we are born again?" Have a member of the class read 1 Corinthians 2:12–13. Write three words on the chalkboard or your overhead transparency, placing them one under the other: *received, know, taught*. Let the group tell you from their student guide the three dimensions of the Holy Spirit's activity once we enter the realm of the invisible kingdom.

3. What is the disciple's assignment when he or she has entered the invisible kingdom? Have someone read Matthew

28:18-20, writing the words highlighted on page 51 on the chalkboard.
4. Now highlight the essential reality of truth in Jesus. Start by writing "disinformation" on the chalkboard or overhead transparency. Ask who uses this tactic (dishonest politicians, people trying to cover a trail of evildoing, the Soviet government). Who is the instigator of disinformation? (Satan, the father of lies.) Who came as the visible manifestation of truth? Read John 18:37.

Facing the Issues

Bring a symbol of God's abundance in nature: a cone, pomegranate, the top of a broccoli plant, a lilac flower, head from a sunflower plant (or a picture of one). Let the class name other examples. Then let them list examples of Jesus' ability to multiply for an abundance during this time on earth.

What gives us as believers access to God's abundance? Read Ephesians 2:4-7. Let someone in the class share an example of God's abundance in his/her life.

How do we enter into partnership with this God of superabundance? Mark 11:23 (preferably the KJV) provides the clue. Discuss the role of the spoken word in making it happen in God's invisible kingdom (pp. 63-65).

Now draw on your research on the use of the word "mind" in the New Testament. Divide the chalkboard or overhead into two columns, listing the negative mindset on the left and the positive mindset on the right. Assign the verses you are using to various members of the class, and let them suggest the truth expressed.

Making It Happen

Write the four key ideas on top of page 69 on the chalkboard or overhead transparency. Then ask: "What are the natural implications for our daily life?"

Ask: "Think of all the negative thinkers you know. What are their truly productive accomplishments?" Now ask for examples of positive thinkers/pray-ers with positive, upbuilding results in their lives.

As you draw to a conclusion, let members of the group list areas where we should be concerned and where positive thinking by Spirit-filled believers can make a difference: internationally, nationally, locally, in your church. Finally, ask them to write down a personal area where they have been thinking negatively, but where the Holy Spirit can help them think/pray positively for superabundant results—the kind you can expect only in the secret kingdom.

If you have people in your group who have not entered the secret kingdom through the new birth, invite them to do so. Offer to spend some time with them personally, possibly at breakfast or lunch, as a way of firming up their commitment.

PROGRESSIVE HAPPINESS

Key Scripture: Matt. 5:3–12

Objectives

1. To determine the conditions for true happiness in the invisible kingdom of God.
2. To gain an understanding of what God is really like from Jesus' teaching in the Beatitudes.
3. To enter into and begin to experience the God-dependency described in the Beatitudes.

Leader Preparation

1. Read Chapter Five in *The Secret Kingdom.*
2. Read Matthew 5, 6, and 7 through in one sitting to get the big picture.

3. Read the Beatitudes in at least three translations.
4. Read the material on Matthew 5:3–12 in one or more commentaries on Matthew or in one of the single-volume Bible commentaries.
5. Do you have someone in your group who has been met by God in an unusually clear demonstration of God meeting us at our point of need? If so, call this person and ask for a testimony of three minutes or less. Use this instead of the illustration in *Setting the Stage*.
6. If you know your group well, write down at least one person per Beatitude who could illustrate it from experience. If necessary, call and forewarn them. Or hand them a slip with the assignment as they enter the class, indicating which Beatitude they are to illustrate from an experience in their life. The goal is to personalize what can be perceived as a totally impractical set of principles.
7. Dr. Robert Coleman, senior professor of evangelism at Asbury Theological Seminary, has said that one of the biblical principles of church growth not mentioned by the American church growth movement is suffering. The role of suffering because of persecution in church growth has been vividly illustrated in this century in the Soviet Union and Communist China. Should you have time, you may want to make an analysis of the role of persecution in the growth of the early church, tying the discussion to Matthew 5:11–12, Acts 5:14; 8:1–4. For context, read chapters 3 through 8 in Acts.

Setting the Stage

If you do not have anyone who can give an illustration of how God meets us at our point of need, you may use the following.

Ode Wannebo had received some of the most glowing accolades given concert artists. His rich bass voice had been heard in some of the finest concert halls of Europe and North America. Yet as he walked the Waikiki Beach the last days of 1971, a deep sense of despair and utter loneliness threatened to overwhelm him. Alcohol addiction had robbed him of the ability to adequately prepare for the concert stage, and the concert that had brought him to Honolulu was set up as only one more effort to help him regain his former glory.

"I reached the end of my rope on New Year's Eve, 1971," he says. "In my hotel room I cried out to God. Suddenly, as if a curtain had been pulled away, God revealed His Son, Jesus Christ, to me. I sank to my knees and stuttered my first prayer in years to a Person I had almost forgotten about. God in His grace met me in my hour of desperation."

Today God is using Ode Wannebo in a unique ministry to Christians with alcohol problems through the Victor's Circle.

Ask: "What does Ode's experience tell us about God?" "What does it tell us about the attitude we need to have if God is to meet us?"

Getting God's Perspective

As a review of what you have already covered, ask: "What is the character of God's invisible kingdom, and what kind of people inhabit it?" The answers are in the first paragraph of page 76.

What is the first activity of a new organization or country? A group writes a constitution. What is the constitution for the invisible kingdom of God? The Sermon on the Mount. It's a good exercise at this point to see how much the group members know about the content of the Sermon on the Mount. Be prepared to write the answers on the chalkboard or overhead transparency. Do not enter into any discussion, simply list and leave, as you mention that the preamble for this constitution is found in Matthew 5:3–12. Let someone read the whole passage.

What is the key that unlocks all the "Blessed" or "Happy is" doors? A deep sense of need. This was true already in the experience of the Old Testament saints. Explain, using the information on page 77.

What does Jesus' name stand for?

The rest of the lesson works well as an interaction between members of the group and you if they have done the work in the Study Guide. If not, try the following.

1. Read Matthew 5:3 and explain the use of the word "poor" as "beggarly." What story did Jesus tell that shows the contrast between the poor in spirit and those who consider themselves rich in spirit? (See Luke 18:13-14.)

2. Read 5:4. What two kinds of mourning should we experience? What progression should we experience? (See middle paragraph of p. 80.) What attitude is an abomination to God? (See Matt. 24:38-39.)

3. Read 5:5. What does the word "meek" mean in everyday language? Then read Numbers 12:3 and ask: "Is Moses the kind of person we would consider meek today?" "Why not?"

4. Read 5:6. According to Galatians 4:4-7, what happens to us when we are born again? Explain the difference between imputed righteousness (Jesus' righteousness is applied to us by God when we by faith accept His death on the cross for us as meeting God's righteous demand) and imparted righteousness (living it out in the here and now). How satisfied shall we be?

5. Read 5:7. What does the word "merciful" really mean? (See 2 Sam. 18:5.)

6. Read 5:8. What will for all time be considered the ultimate happiness of man? When only can we achieve that? Have someone read Matthew 6:24 as an illustration of the necessity to focus fully on God.

7. Read 5:9. What qualifies us to be called sons of God? What is the supreme form of being a peacemaker according to Paul? (See 2 Cor. 5:18-20.)

8. Read 5:10-12. Depending on the amount of time left, do either the study described in point seven under Leader Preparation or ask if anyone has experienced persecution because of his faith in Christ. Have that person share the experience.

Making It Happen

If the class has done the assignments in the Study Guide, ask them to share the prayers they have written. If not, hand out pieces of paper and ask them to write a prayer expressing their desires for their relationship with Christ.

Or you may also want to focus on a specific situation where you as a group or as individuals can be peacemakers. As Christians we often try to stay clear of such troublesome situations because we are afraid of the persecution described in verses 10 through 12. You may want to let some tell their feelings of fear so this can become a point of need where God can become Jehovah-nissi.

UPSIDE DOWN

Key Scripture: 2 Chr. 1:11-12; Rom. 5:1-4; 1 Cor. 13:4-8

Objectives

1. To understand how important humility is to success in the kingdom of God.
2. To grasp how true wisdom from God is dependent on humility.
3. To learn how to implement faith, hope, and love as members of the invisible kingdom.

Leader Preparation

1. As you read Chapter Six in *The Secret Kingdom,* underline or highlight important insights.
2. Read the key Scriptures, including the setting for 2 Chronicles

1:11–12 (read vv. 6–13). Highlight the words "wisdom," "faith," "hope," and "love."

3. Develop a list of people who reveal that "pride goes before a fall." For starters, think of DeLorean, Hitler, Krushchev.
4. All week look for human interest stories in the newspaper and magazines that illustrate faith, hope, and love in action.
5. Try to find someone in your class who illustrates how love can break a cycle of hate or violence.
6. Prepare an overhead transparency with two columns and enter the paradoxes listed on pages 99 and 100.

Setting the Stage

For an effective object lesson, take five equal-sized boxes and write the following words in large letters on the sides of the boxes (one word per box): *wisdom, humility, faith, hope, love, kingdom.*

In class, set the boxes with *wisdom, humility,* and *faith* on the table, leaving a space half the width of a box between the boxes. Now place the boxes with *hope* and *love* over the spaces in the form of a bridge. Bridge the top with the *kingdom* box.

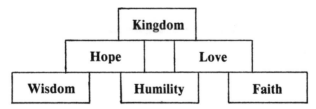

Ask: "Looking at that pyramid of boxes, which virtue is truly foundational to the kingdom of God?" After getting some answers, pull out the box labeled *humility,* thereby collapsing the pyramid.

Now step to the chalkboard or your overhead transparency projector and ask: "What great men and women illustrate the principle I have just demonstrated?"

If you are not able to use boxes, write on the chalkboard or overhead transparency: "God resisteth the proud, but giveth grace to the humble" (1 Pet. 5:5). Ask if the class has found this true in life, drawing out some examples from both history and current events.

Laying the Foundation

Now say: "Considering the significance of humility in the kingdom of God, let's examine what concerns us the most." Ask a member of the group: "What has been of great concern to you during the past months?" Write the answer on the chalkboard or overhead transparency. Repeat the question, directing it at several other members of the class.

Okay, now that the key concerns of the class are in the open, what attitude are we exhorted to have, according to Philippians 2:5–8? Why does Paul go into this discussion? For the answer we need to go back to verses 3 and 4. At this point you can let the class give answers to the questions in the Study Guide.

What attitudes discussed in the previous class session are not displayed by the proud man? Which are displayed by the humble man? (See top of p. 92.)

Paging Mr. Solomon

Hand out sheets of paper and pencils. Bridge to this activity by saying: "Imagine going into church to meditate on Tuesday and hearing the Lord say, 'Tell me what you would really like, and I will give it to you.' Draw the first thing that comes to your mind." Give about two minutes for this. Then say: "Now let's turn to 2 Chronicles 1:6–12 and see what someone else's response was to a similar promise."

Who restated the principle illustrated here many years later in the New Testament? (See Matt. 6:33.)

Now focus on the pattern developed at the bottom of page 93, emphasizing what wisdom leads to. Then ask, "How was the wisdom of God expressed in the Old Testament?" Follow up with, "How does the New Testament believer gain wisdom?"

Lesson from the Garden

What is the expression of the indwelling wisdom of God in the believer?

Draw on an illustration from life. What do you look for in a child from infancy to adolescence (about seventh grade)? Let the class answer. Obedience, most will agree. And we call a child wise if he obeys his parents. But when the child enters adolescence the pattern changes to more independent behavior. Yet again we consider the teen wise if his behavior reflects the patterns of obedience of the childhood years, thus choosing good over evil.

Adam and Eve had no such childhood, so God established a test of obedience that was to set a pattern of obedience in motion. Read Genesis 2:16-17. What was the test of obedience? What would they have become if they had remained obedient? Instead, their disobedience revealed how foolish they were, and they missed out on gaining God's wisdom. Write on the chalkboard or overhead transparency the two statements starting with "For good is..." and "Evil is doing...." (See p. 95.) Conclude with: "What kind of people is God looking for in His invisible kingdom?"

The Big Three

Divide the chalkboard or an overhead transparency into three columns. Write *faith* at the top of the first, *hope* at the top of the second, and *love* at the top of the third column. Write down the characteristics of each virtue, drawing them from pages 95-99. Let the class read Romans 5:1-4 for the biblical basis for faith and hope, and 1 Corinthians 13:4-8 for love.

Point out that when you have *faith* in a Person, Jesus Christ, *hope* based on the moral rightness of God's purpose, you are free to *love* in such a way that this can break the cycle of violence, hate, and destruction.

If you have time, illustrate the power of faith, hope, or love in the natural man. Then point out how much more powerful it becomes in a Holy Spirit empowered person such as Pat Robertson, General Booth of the Salvation Army, Mother Theresa of Calcutta, Bob Pierce of World Vision, and others.

Making It Happen

Divide the group into two and have them read the paradoxes antiphonally, one section reading what the world says and the other what the kingdom says.

Considering all of this, what does Jesus mean in Matthew 5:14? Ask class members to give concrete examples of where they can provide leadership in implementing love expressions in the family, church, community, work environment.

In conclusion ask: "Is it possible to be humble, disciplined, faithful, hopeful, and loving and still provide leadership in today's world?" During the next eight sessions we will study the laws of the kingdom that make it possible.

THE LAW OF RECIPROCITY

Key Scripture: Luke 6:31, 35-38

Objectives

1. To recognize that the Law of Reciprocity is a universal and foundational principle of the kingdom of God.
2. To understand how the Law of Reciprocity can both work for us and against us.
3. To begin to apply the Law of Reciprocity in community and personal relationships.
4. To see how applying the Law of Reciprocity in community and national life will bring the invisible world into action in the visible world.

Leader Preparation

1. Read Chapter Seven in *The Secret Kingdom,* underlining key

ideas. Then reread it to highlight real life illustrations of the universality of the Law of Reciprocity.

2. Make a list of the significant Bible passages included in the chapter, and either read them during your personal devotional time or set aside specific time to meditate on them. The goal is to let God speak to you through His Word.

3. All week look for real life illustrations of the Law of Reciprocity in the magazines and newspapers you read, the television news programs you watch. Be on the alert for situations where the Law of Reciprocity does not apply.

4. In prayer, focus on each one in your group, asking God to bring to your mind how this session could be a life-changing experience for that person. As you do so the Lord may bring to mind one or more who has had an experience that illustrates the Law of Reciprocity. Call them and encourage them to share their experiences during the group session.

5. Read the case study and be prepared to present it at the start of the group session. Do not let the group get into a discussion of possible solutions. These should emerge during the group discussion so that you can discuss a plan of action at the end of the session.

6. Be sure to complete the student lesson so you can provide leadership in the discussion of answers.

7. Prepare an outline for the discussion process so that you will not be tied to the textbook.

Setting the Stage

Read the story in the Study Guide about the congressional election. Then ask: "Should Pat Fleck use his information to raise doubts about the moral character of the congressman?" "Suppose his campaign manager leaked the information, what should Pat do?"

Suggest to the class that you will come back to this case study after the discussion of the Law of Reciprocity.

What Jesus Taught

Many of the world's maxims have been derived from the biblical teaching of past generations. Write the Golden Rule on the chalkboard or overhead transparency and ask: "What makes this law so universally true? Why is it so foundational to all relationships?" For the answer turn to Luke 6:31. The authority of the One who taught it gives it universal application.

If possible, break your group into segments of three or four to discuss the following questions based on Luke 6:31, 35–38: What is the universal principle? What kind of people should we treat as we would like to be treated? What three actions should express our relationship to the Father? What would be the cost, from the natural man's point of view? Who is the guarantor of the Law of Reciprocity? Take five to eight minutes, depending on the length of your session.

The Universal Principle

The universality and foundational nature of the Law of Reciprocity is even expressed in nature. If you have an engineer or a science teacher in the group, ask him to explain the principle by which jet engines and rocket engines work. These engines illustrate that for every action there is an opposite and equal reaction in nature. Is this true in human life as well? Ask someone who has moved around a lot to explain how they establish new friendships in the neighborhood. Then ask for an example in international affairs (the Israeli/PLO attacks and counter-attacks, the Soviet arms build-up in response to the West's arms build-up).

Do not let these discussions degenerate into personal "position papers" on defense strategy. You are merely briefly highlighting examples of the universal principle enunciated by Jesus, using it to focus on the two possible responses described at the bottom of page 105 and top of 106 in the discussion on the Vietnam War.

33

Facing the Issues

From page 109 write the following on the chalkboard or overhead transparency: "If you are in financial trouble, the smartest thing you can do is to start giving money away. Give tithes and offerings to the Lord. Give time. Give work. Give love." Ask: "Is this true? Does it match what the Bible teaches?" Draw a line down the center of the chalkboard or overhead transparency and head one side "What the world says" and the other side "What the Bible says." Let the members of the class give you the world's viewpoint first. Then move through the argument developed by Pat and Bob on pages 106–114.

In his book *Love Unlocks Every Door* Arlis Priest tells of being invited to speak at an assembly in a deep South high school the first day it was open after racial violence. As he walked up to the microphone he did not know what to say, for the students made it very obvious they were not about to listen to him. In what became his trademark, he said, "I love you, and God loves you." Suddenly the talking ceased and students turned to the platform. For forty-five minutes you could have heard a pin drop as he talked about God's love in action. Dozens made commitments for Jesus Christ when he finished. One year later there still had been no recurrence of violence. The Law of Reciprocity had taken effect.

When you have told this story, let a class member tell Pat and Dick Simmons's experience (p. 116). Now ask: "What racial situations in our community need this application of the principle of love in action?" Then ask: "What specifically can you and I do?"

Facing the New Reality

What would happen if we all implemented actions consistent with the Law of Reciprocity? List the key areas presented by Pat on pages 117 and 118. What do we need to make it work in our life? Ask one student to read Matthew 22:39 and another Romans 8:35–37. How do we win over through love? In the strength of Him who loves us! He brings the power of the invisible world to bear on the visible world's problems.

Making It Happen

Now let's return to Pat Fleck's campaign quandary. What should he do about the juicy information he has about the incumbent congressman? What would happen if he or his campaign manager released the information? Who would be hurt most in the mudslinging that would erupt?

During the final two to three minutes ask the class to write down one area in their lives where they need to put Jesus' Law of Reciprocity into action. Suggest they be prepared next session to report on how God implemented the Law of Reciprocity in that specific situation, based on their commitment to implement the Golden Rule of Jesus.

SESSION SIX
THE LAW OF USE

Key Scripture: Matt. 25:14–30

Objectives

1. To understand why God's Law of Use determines success or failure in all areas of life.
2. To understand how the Law of Use, in tandem with the exponential curve, works in all areas of finance—personal, corporate, and government.
3. To motivate group members to take positive steps to take advantage of the exponential-curve effect.

Leader Preparation

1. Read Chapter Eight of *The Secret Kingdom.*
2. Read all the scripture passages in the chapter, focusing on how the Law of Use is illustrated by Jesus Himself.

36

3. Look around your community for examples of the effect of the exponential curve. Examples may be a local businessman, a church that seems to have exploded in recent years, a chain operation of some kind.

4. Look for someone in your class or church who can effectively use a calculator or a portable computer. Introduce this person to the exponential curve and its effect so he can provide some on-the-spot calculations.

5. Evaluate areas in your life where the curve has been going the wrong way because you have not taken advantage of the up-curve effect of the exponential curve.

Setting the Stage

Here are a variety of openers, depending on the age and setting of your groups.

1. If your group tends to be above thirty-five years of age and in an urban environment, you may want to ask, "What happens when a building is empty for a period of time?" You may even want to have a series of slides taken to show empty properties in the area. Conversely, you may have a strong downtown renovation program and could use this to illustrate what happens when people actually make use of property. Do not spend more than three minutes on this.

2. If your group is largely young adults, you may want to call on someone active in an athletic program to illustrate what happens to muscles when they are used. A truly young class may even have a rope-skipping competition between an active person and a not-so-active person. Again, do it only long enough to illustrate the point.

3. If you have a memory practitioner in your group you could let this person illustrate how much we can remember with practice.

4. Move on to a reading of Matthew 25:14–30, pointing out that this parable illustrates through the words of Jesus the Law of Use. Now ask: "What sets the five- and two-talent men apart

37

from the one-talent man?'' The willingness to take a risk. And what does Jesus say about the man unwilling to take a risk? (See vv. 26–27, 30.)

How does Jesus state the Law of Use? (See v. 29.) What does this say to us about the distribution of wealth in our society? About why some physically less-endowed people still excel in athletics? What is the bottom line for us? (See p. 124, the last two paragraphs before the subheading.)

Facing the Issues

What are the three areas of your life in which the Law of Use is effective? Body, mind, and spirit. Taking your cue from the examples given by Pat Robertson, develop some from your group or community.

The Exponential Curve

In your transition to the material on the exponential curve, set a bookkeeper, accountant, or computer specialist at a table on which you place a calculator or a portable computer. Write "$50" on the chalkboard or overhead transparency, telling the class you are going to ask for totals for every five years if you deposited $50 every month at 8 percent interest. If your group can handle a little humor, dramatize the progress, the growth of the deposit. Draw a graph, if possible, showing how the amount suddenly curves upward sharply.

If you are in a farming community, do the above with seed grain, showing the tremendous upward curve if all the grain harvested from one ear of corn or head of wheat or barley were used only as seed.

What is the key to this happening in our lives? What is the trap we so easily fall into? At this point you may want to review the answers in the Study Guide devoted to this section. If you have a pilot or frequent flier, let this person explain the airplane illustration near the bottom of page 128.

Write the clincher for this section on the chalkboard or overhead transparency: "God wants us to have goals that are demanding enough to keep us occupied, but are not overtaxing, and to stick with them long enough for them to come to fruition" (p. 129). As illustration have members read Matthew 13:31–32 and Mark 4:26–29.

Now draw on the abilities and skills in the class to firm up this point in the minds of group members, pointing to examples where persistence led to accomplishment.

Wrong Side of the Curve

Introduce the negative results of the exponential curve by asking, "If the curve goes up, can it also go down?" As an illustration, consider what has happened in the educational system of some of the states in the United States. Lack of emphasis on basics and a focus on electives resulted in graduates without basic skills in math and reading. In a 1983 test of teachers applying for certification, about one-third failed to pass new basic language and math tests. In past years these teachers simply moved into the classroom and taught. One generation of such teachers produced a generation of functional illiterates, who then became teachers and produced even more poorly educated students. Without drastic action the whole educational system could return to the primitive level despite computers in offices and homes.

What has happened in personal and government finances? Discuss what Pat Robertson touches on in the section on page 130.

Read all of Matthew 4:1–11 if you have time. If not, tell of Jesus' temptation and ask, "What did Satan really want to achieve with Jesus?" You may get the standard answer, "pride." Though true, the appeal to pride was couched in the "you can have it now" aspect of the temptation.

Since man is incurably addicted to "I want it now," what provision did God make to halt the downward curve in Israel? Read Deuteronomy 23:19. Refer back to the effect of compound interest in your opening example for this section.

How did God try to restore balance in Israel? Read Leviticus

39

25:8-10. What implications does this have for us today? (See p. 133.)

Making It Happen

By way of review, point to the all-pervasive impact of the Law of Reciprocity. Then indicate the powerful nature of the Law of Use, coupled with the exponential curve. Why is it so important? Write answers down on the overhead transparency or on the chalkboard. After you have covered the principle of increasing opportunity, ask members of the class to list specific situations in the church and community where this could be applied. Then ask them to write down the opportunity in their lives that could explode under the impact of the Law of Use and the exponential curve. If you have a small group, ask members to share what they have written down as a way of confirming by public statement their determination to implement the Law of Use.

THE LAW OF PERSEVERANCE

Key Scripture: Matt. 7:7–11; Luke 11:5–8; 18:1–8

Objectives

1. To lay hold of Christ's teaching on perseverance.
2. To become aware of the tactics of the enemy in his attempts to discourage and depress us, short-circuiting perseverance.
3. To determine areas of life where perseverance is needed to bring the benefits of the invisible kingdom to reality in the visible world.

Leader Preparation

1. Read and highlight Chapter Nine in *The Secret Kingdom*. This is a short chapter, so the key ideas will need more development.

2. Make a deliberate effort to accumulate true stories of how perseverance paid off. Look for examples in your community, state, and nation. For example, even though you may disagree with him politically, you have to admire Jimmy Carter's perseverance in seeking the presidency in the mid-1970s, culminating with his election as president in 1976.

3. Read the key Scriptures, adding the stories of Jacob wrestling with God (see Gen. 32:24–29), and Paul's statements about his perseverance (see 2 Cor. 4:7–18).

4. Develop an outline for your classroom presentation, integrating answers from the Study Guide.

5. Pat Robertson uses the example of a chick pecking its way through the shell of the egg. If you know of other examples of perseverance in nature, prepare to present them in the Setting the Stage opener.

Setting the Stage

Highlight examples of perseverance in nature and natural man—the expedition that climbed Mt. Everest, the desert yucca plant that grows for seven years to produce one flowering stalk, an animal determined to get on the other side of a fence, the pianist who practices six to eight hours a day for years to achieve concert level excellence. Then ask: "What do we learn from these examples about the nature of success?" Point out that Jesus also highlighted the need for perseverance again and again. He knew there are no easy roads to genuine maturity in the kingdom of God.

Facing the Issues

The Necessity of Effort. Let a member of the group read Matthew 7:7–11. What is the obvious lesson usually drawn from this statement of Jesus? What do we miss if we stay at that level? The need to persist in prayer is built on the foundation of the underlying principle, the Law of Perseverance. Suggest that you can see this principle illustrated every day in a supermarket, where children's "Can I have..." requests wear down innumerable parents.

Either on your chalkboard or overhead transparency write the simple English statements *ask, seek,* and *knock* vertically. Beside them write the actual Greek tense used, expressed as *keep asking, keep seeking,* and *keep knocking.*

Consider what application Matthew 11:12 has to perseverance.

The Necessity of Struggle. Ask how this compares with some of the current Christian teaching on speaking the word of faith. What does this teaching overlook?

How long did Jacob struggle with God? (See Gen. 32:24-29.)

How long was Moses in the wilderness with the children of Israel? Forty years!

How long was God's school of obedience for Judah in Babylonian captivity?

How long was the struggle for independence in the United States? Even though the patriots believed in the cause, the struggle lasted seven years, for they were up against greedy merchants and lords in England.

How long does it take to translate the New Testament into the language of a tribe in today's world? One Wycliffe team has been at it for more than forty years with a tribe in Mexico.

If we cannot expect things to happen at a snap of a finger, why are we encouraged to have faith, to believe God is going to act? One of the reasons is found in Luke 18:1-8. Why did the widow have to keep at her request so long? She was dealing with the natural attitudes of people in the visible world. What force from the invisible world do we bring into the struggle when we persist in prayer? (See Luke 18:7.)

Perseverance demands the willingness to struggle.

The Necessity of Conflict. Yet what is the natural tendency of all of us? To counteract that, read Luke 11:5-8. Remind the group of the Syro-Phoenician woman (see Matt. 15:21-28) who persisted in asking for her daughter's healing even though Jesus clearly seemed unwilling to do so. Can you imagine how the disciples may have felt at her seeming impertinence?

Yet conflict and suffering have ever been the experience of the

43

church. Read Acts 14:22 to illustrate the attitude Paul encouraged in the early church. Interestingly, John Mark was no longer with Paul and Barnabas at this point, even though he had started the trip with them. Read what he did in Acts 13:13 and what it showed to Paul in chapter 15:38.

Thus the pressure that conflict brings is not necessarily a negative factor in our lives but an opportunity to persevere in the power of God. Point to the experience of the contemporary church in the Soviet Union and Red China.

The Necessity of Being Alert. Discuss the negative thoughts Satan pours into our minds. If you discuss suicide you may want to refer to King Saul in the Old Testament. Draw on the experience of Elijah in 1 Kings 19 to illustrate that a great triumph does not mean we are free of Satan's temptation to depression.

Have a group member read 2 Corinthians 4:7–10 and ask: "What is the difference between Elijah's experience and the apostle Paul's experience?" Paul drew on the power of the invisible kingdom in the person of the indwelling Christ to overcome in the visible kingdom. (See also 1 Cor. 10:13; 2 Tim. 1:12.)

Perseverance Pays Off

Present contemporary examples of perseverance from your group, community, and nation to personalize the examples given by Pat Robertson.

Making It Happen

You live in an unincorporated area next to a medium-size city, which has been extending its borders in a haphazard manner for some years. Because of rapid growth in housing in your area it would appear best to attempt to gain self-government through incorporation as another city. What will you need to do to achieve that goal? Discuss a potential strategy.

Your church would like to start a camp in a nearby mountain area. What will it take to develop the facilities needed?

Your husband or wife is not a believer. What kind of praying will be necessary?

If none of these particularly apply, tackle a really tough problem in your church or community and discuss what kind of action will be needed to have the Law of Perseverance take effect.

Wrap-up

"Keep on asking, He said, keep on seeking, and keep on knocking. Don't be afraid even to make a ruckus. God prefers that to slothfulness and indolence. He wants people who will travail and perhaps stumble a bit, but keep on going forward" (p. 140).

SESSION EIGHT
THE LAW OF RESPONSIBILITY

Key Scripture: Is. 58:1–11; Luke 12:42–48; 1 Tim. 3:1–7

Objectives
1. To recognize that if we have been given much by God we have a corresponding level of responsibility to use our gifts.
2. To think through how the Law of Responsibility affects us in the church, society, and the nation and is an integral part of our free enterprise system.
3. To develop an awareness of conditions in our community that call for a responsible response.

Leader Preparation

1. Read Chapter Ten in *The Secret Kingdom,* highlighting how the Law of Responsibility affects the church, society, the nation, and our economic system.
2. Read the Scripture used in the chapter, drawing out personal applications to help you transfer ideas into actions.

46

3. Look for examples of irresponsible actions in the church, society, and the nation. For example, consider the flight of evangelical churches to the suburbs, leaving the inner city to God's adversary. Or consider the bankruptcy rate among banks because of greed—over-extension on high-risk loans. Possibly you know of companies who fired employees with thirty or forty years of service just because they were nearing retirement age. Or the irresponsible actions of law-and-order people who want tougher prison terms but vote down bond issues for increased prison facilities.
4. You may want to be ready with an overhead transparency to compare the excesses in both socialism and capitalism that disqualify them as God's ideal economic system (a two-column chart on the chalkboard is an alternative). Then you can highlight under what conditions capitalism is acceptable.
5. Be ready to break the group into segments of three to four for a study of Isaiah 58:1–11, giving each a list of two questions: What did God's people do that displeased Him? What similar conditions in our community should be tackled by us as Christians?

Setting the Stage

If your group has a few musicians, tackle the Artur Rubinstein quote (p. 145). If you have a number of tennis players, use the tennis illustration. Some groups might relate to the example of the Art DeMoss family in Pennsylvania, who own a large home in one of the prestigious areas on the outskirts of Philadelphia. Their home became a byword for hospitality, even though they could have selfishly maintained it for their own use. Missionaries, a traveling Christian rock group, businessmen from all parts of the world were welcomed in the name of Christ. Though Art is now with the Lord, the family continues an extensive outreach through evangelistic dinners. A family foundation also channels large amounts of money to various Christian enterprises around the world as an expression of responsible use of income.

Now have members of the group read Luke 12:42–48.

THE SECRET KINGDOM: LEADER'S GUIDE

If you find a significant example of irresponsibility in the newspaper or newsmagazines, you may want to use that as a class opener, particularly if it is a story with strong emotional appeal. Then read the Luke passage.

Facing the Issues

Highlight some of the "much has been given" in your group to help them realize that even if we are poor by North American standards, we are rich by Third World standards. So the passage applies to us today.

You may want to ask: "Yet why, if the Law of Responsibility is biblical, do many people succeed without obeying it?" The answer is that "Exercise of the Law of Use will bring success, especially if done in tandem with the Law of Perseverance" (p. 145). Yet if we really want the power of the invisible kingdom active in the visible world, we need to exercise responsibility with the rewards of that success.

The Church

What are some of the areas in the church where the Law of Responsibility must be practiced? (See James 3:1; 1 Tim. 3:1-7.)

What had the early disciples of Christ been given that loaded them with such a high level of responsibility? (See Mark 4:11.) How does Paul feel about it? (See Rom. 1:14.) What about us ordinary Joes? (See 1 Tim. 3:15.) Conclude with Jesus' final words in Matthew 28:18-20.

The Society and the Nation

As Americans, thinking positively about British colonialism is a rare occurrence. So the group may have difficulty with Pat Robertson's extensive overview of *noblesse oblige,* especially if they have seen the film "Gandhi." If you have someone with historical knowledge, have this person develop this section, even if only the segment on the United States is treated. You may find considerable disagreement in your class over some of Pat Robertson's statements on America's lack of leadership in keeping the peace. Events in the Mideast and Central America will have advanced considerably by the time you teach.

The key statement for this section is at the top of page 151. You may want to write the section beginning with, "For multi-faceted..." and ending with "...duty that accompany it" on the chalkboard or overhead and use it as an "umbrella" statement to guide the discussion.

The Issue of Capitalism

Ask: "What economic system most nearly meets the need for freedom?" Then do the chart described in section four of Leader Preparation.

What are some unhealthy manifestations of greed in the community you live in? In your state?

What should produce an acknowledgment of responsibility to God? (See top of p. 153.) Yet what have conservative evangelicals traditionally focused on to the exclusion of other responsibilities? You may want to point to positive examples of assuming responsibility, such as that evidenced by CBN, John Perkins and the Voice of Calvary Ministries, the various involvements in outreach to the needy in Haiti, World Vision, Compassion, etc.

Making It Happen

Break the group into segments of three or four, handing each group the two questions based on Isaiah 58:1–11 given in section five of Leader Preparation.

Remind the group in conclusion that learning new truth adds a new layer of responsibility, which demands obedience if we want to receive God's blessing.

Wrap-up

"Give, and it will be given to you. Fulfill your responsibility at your current level if you would rise to a higher one. Blessing carries responsibility" (p. 155).

THE LAW OF GREATNESS

Key Scripture: Matt. 18:1-4; Luke 22:24-27

Objectives

1. To understand why becoming truly great depends on becoming like a child and being a servant.
2. To grasp how being like a child and a servant works at all levels of life.
3. To learn how to implement being trusting, teachable, and humble as a lifestyle.

Leader Preparation

1. Read Chapter Eleven in *The Secret Kingdom* and highlight what it means to be like a child and a servant.
2. Read the Scripture referred to and memorize Luke 22:26.

3. Become thoroughly familiar with the biography of one of the men or women referred to by Pat Robertson so you can draw on that person's example more fully in class. You may desire to use someone else as a role model, such as Wayne Alderson, whose story is told in *Stronger Than Steel: The Wayne Alderson Story.*

4. Make a list of people probably familiar to the class who illustráte being trusting, teachable, humble, and willing to serve. And keep an eye open for examples in the newspaper and newsmagazines.

5. Prepare a sample case history that you can type on an overhead transparency that portrays a tough life situation. Prepare three discussion questions that can be tackled by small groups of three or four. The idea is to work toward a solution using the principles undergirding the Law of Greatness.

Setting the Stage

Either put on the overhead transparency or hand out the case history developed in number five above. If you do not have one, you may want to present the story about the bus driver in the Study Guide. Ask the members of the group to share their thoughts about John's problem.

Suggest that the class keep this example in mind as you study the Law of Greatness, since you'll come back to it under Making It Happen. Then you'll want to apply what you have learned about true greatness to John's situation. Remember, and then highlight the material at the bottom of page 156.

Facing the Issues

Have you ever heard children or teens arguing over who is the greatest athlete in one of the sports, or who is the greatest actor or popular singer? What are some of the arguments you might hear? List them on the chalkboard or overhead transparency. Now read about a similar discussion by the disciples of Jesus in Matthew 18:1–4.

Ask: "What is the criterion for greatness established by Jesus in this incident?" For contrast read Luke 22:24–27. What additional criterion does Jesus set forth here? Put all the criteria on the chalkboard or overhead transparency.

Now place yourself in a union hall. What would be the reaction of the men if you set forth these criteria for greatness?

Becoming like a Child

What three qualities of a child are highlighted by Pat Robertson?

How does being trusting contribute to greatness? (Compare 1 Cor. 13:7; Phil. 4:19.)

What characteristics of teachableness lead to greatness? (See middle of p. 159.)

How does a child manifest humility? He loves people, loves life, is free to engage himself fully. Highlight the three characteristics in the second paragraph on page 160. Think of people who today illustrate these characteristics (Charles Swindoll and Joyce Landorf in their books, for example). Have someone read Matthew 23:12, moving on to Proverbs 22:4 and the three things men long for.

Conclude with the circle described by Pat Robertson near the bottom of page 160.

Being a Servant

Read Luke 22:24–27 again for a major criterion for greatness. You could start this session by asking what it is about people like Albert Schweitzer and Mother Theresa that appeals to people so much, and then move into the passage of Scripture.

How does this square with the widely held belief that in today's world you must "look out for No. 1"? What kinds of people may have difficulty with the concept of being a servant?

For an elaboration of this whole section, read *Improving Your Serve,* by Charles Swindoll. He has some excellent anecdotes from personal experience. You may also be able to highlight the service to communities across America provided by the "700 Club" and CBN as one way in which Pat Robertson is fulfilling his vision for service.

A Case in Point

Pat Robertson presents a comparison between the American and Japanese auto industry in their attitudes toward service. You may have someone able to show a similar negative pattern in England, where the unions adopted an attitude of "Give us what we want, or we'll strike!" The result was economic chaos. If you read *Man of Steel* you may want to highlight the development of an attitude of service under the leadership of Wayne Alderson.

Making It Happen

Divide your group into segments of three or four and ask them to answer the following questions: As a union member, where can John promote a climate of trust, teachableness, and humility? If this attitude were to grow and take hold, what kind of an influence might it have on deliberations regarding the future of the bus service? How can John demonstrate the attitude of a servant? What effect might this have on the attitude of management and city government?

As an alternative, let members of the class write out one situation where they can exhibit the characteristics of greatness, in contrast to the pettiness so often evident in today's society. Then close in a special prayer of commitment to model Christ's lifestyle of servanthood.

THE LAW OF UNITY

Key Scripture: Gen. 1:26, 11:6–8; Matt. 18:19–20; John 17:20–23; Acts 13:1–3; 1 Cor. 12:4–7

Objectives

1. To understand that since God is a unity, unity is central to the way the world works.
2. To recognize how unity unleashes the power of God in the individual, the group, the church, and the nation.
3. To understand how diversity can exist within unity.
4. To work toward unity of purpose individually and as a group.

Leader Preparation

1. Read and highlight key ideas in Chapter Twelve of *The Secret Kingdom.*

2. This chapter has an abundance of Scripture, so be sure to read all passages within their context first, then in connection with the setting in the chapter.

3 An excellent passage to memorize is 1 Corinthians 12:4–7, since it highlights both the unity of God and the diversity of the Spirit's expression, all focused on a common goal.

4. Clip newspaper examples of both unity and disunity. You may even want to paste a larger number of headlines revealing disunity in your community and the nation on a large sheet of white paper. Place it on a wall or table so early arrivals to class will be able to study it.

5. If you have a group member whose family exhibits strong unity in a social, business, political, or church environment, ask this person to share his/her secret for family unity.

6. A picture puzzle exemplifies diversity in unity, so you may want to put together a smaller one with larger pieces so you can hold it in an almost vertical position for the class.

7. Unless you have the outline clearly in mind, this lesson could easily get bogged down because it has more points than usual. So be sure you have a clear outline in front of you as you lead.

Setting the Stage

Start by drawing attention to an example of disunity stifling progress in a local, state, or national government setting. Then compare this with the unity forged by President Reagan during the budget sessions of 1982. What was the difference in results?

Now move to Genesis 1:26 and ask, "Where do we find the most powerful example of unity and its effect?" Then have someone read the passage. What may have been the "us" referred to in this Scripture?

Highlight the Key Idea in the Study Guide, pointing out how not only creative power flowed from God's unity but also, as revealed in Genesis 3:22–23, judgment. What justification do we have for believing this powerful unity also works on earth? (See Matt. 6:10; 18:19–20.) How does the exponential curve affect the Law of Unity?

The Law in Action

What was the secret of the exponential growth of the early church? (See Acts 1:14; 13:1–3.)

What will prevent unbelievers from hearing the message of the gospel? Have an illustration ready from the contemporary church.

How can unity develop into a negative force? Give the example from Genesis 11. What motivated the unity in building the Tower of Babel? When and how have we seen similar unity at work negatively? In the strength of Nazi Germany under Hitler, the Islamic revival in Iran, the Gay Rights movement in San Francisco, the united attack upon any expression of Christianity in public by the American Civil Liberties Union.

Can such expressions of negative unity scare even believers? Why should they not scare us? (See top of p. 173.) Add specific Scripture verses such as Philippians 4:13.

Facing the Issues

Can the individual really make a difference? Unity must happen in the individual, the society, the nation; and the individual is part of all those. What is the key to the individual "getting it all together?" (See James 1:6). How does Abraham illustrate this? (See Rom. 4:13–21; Ps. 57:7.)

Let some of the class members share what happened when they developed a single purpose in their lives.

Do use the example of Mary and Martha, for we do not get too many examples that have such a clear significance for the homemaker.

If it is tough as a single homemaker to have a single focus, how about the wife determined to make her husband No. 1 in her life? How can a husband put Christ first in his life and keep his relationship to his wife in balance? Try again to get some sharing from the class on what happens when the focus is wrong.

The key sentence to highlight either by writing it on a chalkboard or on an overhead transparency is: "Single-mindedness is the solution to the internal desperation so many people regularly experience" (p. 175).

A Collective Principle

What is the difference between Israel and Lebanon during the last fifteen years? Why has Israel defeated all attempts to overrun it, while Lebanon became home for the PLO and Syrian troops? Lebanon, like Italy before the days of Garibaldi, is an example of a country divided by many little "kingdoms."

What did Jesus say about this? (See Matt. 12:25.)

Discuss this principle in terms of family, with reference to the Kennedy family and a local family.

If you have a business person in the group, let him/her tell how this is illustrated in business.

Pat Robertson discusses Italy as an example of a disunited country (p. 177). You could probably add France, with its history of strong Socialist and Communist influence, and the student riots of 1958 and 1968, which helped topple the government of that day.

What made the United States different until the 1960s? Why are we experiencing such widespread disunity at all levels of government?

A Caution

What attitude do we need to guard against when we promote unity? You may want to list some of the disciples, letting the class suggest the character types represented. An example of diversity in unity from nature is water, which appears as water, vapor, and ice. Water has a variety of characteristics, depending on temperature and pressure.

What does the apostle Paul say? (See 1 Cor. 12:4–7.)

Making It Happen

Encourage members of the group to share what they put into the Study Guide about a personal, highly focused goal in life, and how their goals can give new unity to their lives. Compare with what the apostle Paul did (see Phil. 3:12–14).

Invite the group to suggest a unifying activity (praying for an unsaved friend or relative in the group, reaching out to a specific poor family, sharing as a group in an outreach program in the church).

If you have several businessmen, ask them to contribute their company's purpose in one sentence. If you are not getting much action, work up one together.

Your church may not have a unifying purpose. Work at writing the purpose of your church in one sentence.

What was Jesus' prayer in John 17:20–23? Discuss how this can become a reality in your immediate circle of influence.

THE LAW OF MIRACLES

Key Scripture: Num. 13:1–14:10; 1 Sam. 14:1–15; Mark 10:27; 11:25–26; John 14:12; Rom. 4:20–21; 1 Cor. 12:8–10

Objectives

1. To accept that God will override the natural order when the principles governing the Law of Miracles are in place.
2. To understand how the Law of Miracles can bring the power of the invisible world into reality in the visible world.
3. To grasp what the major hindrances are to God's working through miracles.
4. To let the personal examples motivate group members to employ the principles that will make God's miracle power accessible to them.

Leader Preparation

1. Read Chapter Thirteen of *The Secret Kingdom,* highlighting key ideas.
2. Read all the key Scriptures, plus the passages listed in the foot-notes on page 185.
3. Make a separate study of the passages where Jesus spoke a command in the performing of a miracle.
4. If "speaking out" is a new concept to you, activate this prac-tice in your life in an area where you have long had a secret desire that God would act.
5. Alert members of your group in advance if you know they have experienced God's miracle-working power in their lives, urg-ing them to share what God has done for them.
6. Prepare one faith goal for your group which requires God to perform a miracle if it is to be reached. This may relate to a member of the group (the reconciliation of a husband or wife with a separated spouse), to the group as a whole (claiming a friend or relative of the group for salvation), to the church (setting a growth goal considered unachievable except by God blessing an outreach effort in a dramatic way). Be very specific once you have determined the faith goal under the guidance of the Holy Spirit.
7. Develop an outline that includes all the key points in the chapter.

Setting the Stage

Open the group session with the university miracle described on pages 195–197. After telling the story, ask the group a series of questions:
1. What are the extraordinary events in this story that could be characterized as miracles?
2. Why do you think God was able to intervene in Pat Robert-son's life in such a direct way?

THE SECRET KINGDOM: LEADER'S GUIDE

3. What actions growing out of faith made the miracles possible?
4. What indications are there that God had had this miracle in His mind a long time?

Again remember that these questions are not to lead to discussion. They are designed to raise the issues covered in the chapter in such a way that group members will be able to tie the principles to a real happening. You as leader should also be doing this by referring to the illustration repeatedly.

The Rules of Miracles

Present the material on page 181.

What is the umbrella condition for entering the world of miracles? What three attitudes govern activity as a member of the invisible world, the secret kingdom? Step to the chalkboard or use an overhead transparency to list these (*believe, trust, expect*) from page 182.

Now focus on the two rules of the world of miracles, highlighting the Joshua and Caleb attitudes versus the attitudes of the people and the other ten spies. For a positive role-model move to Jonathan. Have class members read relevant segments of the passages involved. Then ask for class participation by questions like: "What was the difference between the attitude of Joshua and Caleb and that of the other spies?" "What did they see compared to the others?" "Why were they willing to move forward despite full awareness of the obstacles?" Similar questions apply to the Jonathan action of faith.

Now list the second rule of miracles. Ask: "What is the precondition if God is to perform miracles through us?" (See last paragraph on p. 183). Let a class member read Romans 4:20–21 and ask: "How strongly must we be convinced that God will act?" Give the contemporary role-model of Pat Robertson and RCA. What indication do we have that such "impossibilities" are often only in our mind? See Mark 10:27.

Conclude with personal examples from class members.

62

The Time to Speak

What turns our faith, our single-minded focus on God's acting, into reality? Have class members read Matthew 8:3; 13; 9:23–25; Mark 4:39; 9:25. Ask: What is the one thing Jesus did in every situation? What is the message for us today? Briefly expand on the last paragraph on page 185.

When should we "continue in prayer" after having spoken out what we are convinced is God's will?

How does speaking out in the name of Christ affect our speech as Christians? What power do we have in our mouths?

The Major Hindrance

Notice the significance Pat Robertson attaches to the lack of forgiveness, to resentment, by the amount of space given this discussion compared to the role of speaking it out. Your group can easily get sidetracked on the role of the tongue and speech, so be sure to move on to this section promptly.

You may want to bridge to this segment by saying: "Okay, we have emphasized the role of faith, highlighted the rules of miracles, and described the significance of speaking out what God has laid on our hearts. What is the biggest hindrance to God now doing a miracle in our lives?" Have someone read Mark 11:25–26 and ask: "What is God's attitude toward our unwillingness to forgive someone?"

Give each person a piece of paper. Ask them to write down the names of people against whom they hold a grudge, people they may even hate, people they know in their heart of hearts they need to forgive for something. Ask them to fold the paper and hold it in their hand. Now ask someone to read 1 John 2:10–11; 3:15. How serious does God consider unforgiveness?

Now read 1 John 1:7–9. Does the speaking out also apply to gaining forgiveness for our unforgiving hearts? Tell the group that if they are willing to seek God's forgiveness for their stubborn pride in not forgiving another, they need to say it in their minds, then tear up the piece of paper. Give a minute of silence while people are bowed before God. Then say: "Now go out after this class and either go to the person or write a letter speaking out your willingness to forgive them."

Depending on the time available you may want to first present the material on page 188. The important thing is to initiate some kind of action that will release God's power. Some dramatic things have happened when people followed through on the above procedure.

The other side of the coin of forgiveness is active love. Let the group read Matthew 22:37–40 and discuss God's command as restated by Jesus.

The illustration on page 190 may be supplemented by one from your group.

Making It Happen

On pages 192–196 Pat Robertson gives examples of God's miracle-working power in his life. These are designed to illustrate the availability of the miracle power of the invisible world for the visible world. As he emphasizes, "All the gifts of the Spirit are exceedingly important when springing from faith, hope, and love." This is demonstrated by 1 Corinthians 12:8–10. You need to determine, as guided by the Holy Spirit, what to achieve in the life of your group's members as you bring the session to a close. One approach is to introduce a faith goal that God has laid on your heart—or let group members express a faith goal—that would require a miracle. Speak it out, write it down, and expect God to act.

As the group is dismissed, remind them to clear up any unforgiveness that will hinder God from unleashing his power.

Wrap-up

"Our principle weapon in the crises we face in the world is love, and love operates only in a state of forgiveness and reconciliation" (p. 189).

THE LAW OF DOMINION

Key Scripture: Gen. 1:26–30; Matt. 24:14; Luke 9:1–2; 1 Cor. 3:5–9; Eph. 6:10–18; 2 Tim. 1:7; Heb. 2:6–15

Objectives

1. To recognize that God has called us to have dominion and subdue the earth, exercising authority as God's fellow-workers.
2. To understand that the sin and rebellion in the Garden of Eden robbed man of access to God's authority, but that Christ's death and resurrection restored that access by faith in Jesus Christ.
3. To learn how to overcome the timidity and discouragement that Satan uses to prevent us from exercising our God-given authority over nature, man, and Satan.
4. To see how a willingness to exercise our authority under the Law of Dominion will result in God's intervention in keeping with the Law of Miracles.

Leader Preparation

1   Read Chapter Fourteen of *The Secret Kingdom* and highlight the key concepts developed by the authors.
2.   Read the Key Scriptures, since these put specific verses used in their larger context.
3.   Memorize a verse that expresses the Law of Dominion in a positive way (e.g., Phil. 4:13; 2 Tim. 1:7).
4.   If you have a small group, have someone collect enough current magazines so that every group member will have one. Bring enough scissors so one in three can use one. If your group is too large for this, clip examples of man's slavery to pleasure, plants, and animals to use in Setting the Stage.
5.   Check the Study Guide for questions and ideas you can use in your interaction with the group.
6.   Make a chart with two columns, heading the first one SLAVERY TO and the second FREEDOM LOST. In the first column list things such as plants, animals—whatever in the environment enslaves man. In the second column write out what freedoms are lost by the specific enslavement. Place it on an overhead transparency or on the chalkboard.

This chapter has fewer real life examples, so call on group members who can give a testimony about a situation where they exercised dominion and subdued the Enemy.

Setting the Stage

If your group is under forty in number, you may want to enlist a couple in bringing enough magazines for each person, plus scissors. Hand out the magazines, then have the group divide into groups of three. Give each group one scissor and ask them to cut out examples of slavery to things, pleasure, plants, animals. Give them between five and ten minutes to do this. Then ask them to hold up examples of articles and name the enslaving object.

An alternative is to cut out headlines and pictures illustrating enslaving objects, lifting them up for the class to see. Then comment on them. Or if you have a corkboard, tack them onto that. Begin the lesson with, "Now that we have illustrated the ways we as humans let ourselves be enslaved, let's read what God had in mind for us when He created us." Have someone read Genesis 1:26–30. Ask the group to describe what God's role was for man when He created us. Highlight the Law of Dominion.

Expressing Dominion

Imagine Adam striding through the Garden of Eden, the words of God ringing in his ears. How did he express dominion over all things? (See Gen. 2:15–20.) In this atmosphere God placed Adam's helpmate, Eve. What resulted in the breakdown of the authority God had given man?

Now move into the authors' description of the words "dominion" and "subdue."

What has God done to help man regain the authority lost by Adam and Eve? (See Heb. 2:14–15.) The return of the power and authority through Jesus Christ makes it possible for man to again "order the planet according to God's will and purpose" (see middle of p. 200).

Why has this not happened? (See p. 201.) What does God desire for man today?

Expressing Subjection

The authors describe a specific subjection to nature on pages 201–203. Introduce this section by asking: "What are some of the specific examples of man's failing to express dominion and actually subjecting himself to nature?" Use the chart described in Setting the Stage, number 6.

The key to man's subjection to nature is his loss of relationship with God. What specifically is the result? (See the top of p. 203.)

What kind of freedom will alone help man to recover authority and dominion? Let a group member read John 8:31-32. And rather than read only Hebrews 2:14-15, take the larger context provided by verses 6-15. This sets forth man's created role, and how through the exaltation of Jesus Christ we become heirs to His authority. It is this identification of the believer with Christ and His authority as the exalted Christ that frees man to resume dominion.

Ask: "If we have this authority to have dominion and subdue nature, can we exercise it in respect to what man calls natural disasters?" The focus for this discussion can be provided by the authors' discussion of it at the bottom of page 203.

The Key Concept

Have group members read Mark 16:20, 1 Corinthians 3:9, and 2 Corinthians 5:20; 6:1. Ask the group what expression common to all passages expresses our new relationship with Jesus Christ. Yet that is still not fully expressive of what this means for us, and it must be taken in connection with 2 Timothy 2:12. When was this exemplified? (See Luke 9:1-2.) And to whom does this authority and power extend? (Compare Matt. 28:18-19; Luke 10:19.) After you have quoted the clinching sentence on the bottom of page 206, ask for examples from the recent past to illustrate this power and authority.

Satan's Strategy

You may want to illustrate Satan's strategy with an example such as the following.

George and Sue (not their real names) had left their daughter in Miami on her way to a summer assignment in Central America. Stopping at Boca Raton for what they hoped would be a relaxing weekend, they discovered their front tires had worn through to the steel cord. When George returned at noon on Saturday his wife was clearly depressed.

"Everything is going wrong," she fumed. "First you forget your garment bag and I forget my shoe bag when we leave. Now this."

Even a lovely afternoon at the beach did not seem to help. By Sunday morning George knew it was time to move on. Arriving in St. Augustine, they toured the old city. Again trouble set in—the restaurants were too crowded, and a family restaurant upset Sue because it had filthy restrooms.

Monday's travel became a silent ordeal as George tried unsuccessfully to break through the deep depression of his wife. At the first stop he brought the Bible into the car, giving it to Sue and challenging her to read the Psalm she had given their daughter in parting. She slammed the Bible on the seat.

Midafternoon Sue suddenly came alive. She began to sing, to become aware of the beautiful countryside. George was pleased, but puzzled. That evening Sue finally was able to share what had happened.

"We were driving over a bridge when I had the strongest urge to take the Bible and throw it into the river. At that point I realized that it was Satan who had caused my depression by constantly telling me, 'All the things that have happened to you are a fulfillment of your father's prediction that God will punish you all your life for your rebellion as a teenager.' I had believed him. So at that point I said to him, 'Satan, you have no part of me. I belong to Jesus Christ. I demand that you leave me alone in the name of Jesus.' And he left me immediately. My depression was gone!"

After presenting this illustration ask: "What are some of the other tactics Satan uses to gain dominion over us? What are some examples of timidity, of embarrassment at being a Christian?"

Ask group members to read 2 Timothy 1:7 and then move to Matthew 24:14.

How did Sue gain dominion over Satan? She mentally verbalized it. Even more effective is to speak it aloud, as Christ did.

Making It Happen

What is the first step in implementing the Law of Dominion? Write it on the chalkboard or overhead transparency: "Before the world can be freed from bondage, man must be made free from himself." How does that happen? (See John 8:31–32.) Remind the group: "When man, through Jesus, reasserts God's dominion over himself, then he is capable of reasserting his God-given dominion over everything else" (p. 203). You may want to lead in a period of quiet commitment at this time.

Remember, we are "workers together with Him." Specifically, what does this mean in terms of personally enslaving habits, of timidity, of unwillingness to confront the Enemy?

As a final step, focus on an area affecting the group or church where dominion, authority in the name of Christ, has been lost or needs to be displayed. As a group, determine what steps of faith need to be taken to go on the offensive to establish the dominion of Christ.

THE COMING KING

Key Scripture: Ezek. 38:1—39:8; Matt. 13:24-43; Luke 8:9-10; 1 Cor. 15:22-28, 48-50; Eph. 1:9-10; 2 Tim. 2:11-13; Heb. 12:25-29; Rev. 13:16-17; 19; 20:1-10; 21:1-5

Objectives

1. To recognize that from the beginning of time God has been intent on establishing a kingdom of people who will voluntarily live under His sovereignty and enjoy His creation.
2. To understand that there will be a time of massive upheaval and realignments of political power before Christ reestablishes His invisible kingdom in a visible way.
3. To grasp that, as believers, we can be part of the *invisible* kingdom now but we will reign with Christ when He comes again to establish His kingdom in a *visible* way.
4. To rejoice in the hope that the Evil One will be vanquished and Christ will be King of Kings and Lord of Lords.

5. To initiate a plan of action designed to bring the invisible world into action in the visible one in obedience to Christ.

Leader Preparation

1. Read and highlight Chapter Fifteen of *The Secret Kingdom.*
2. This session is undergirded by more Scripture than any other, so be prepared to take more time than usual to read all the passages, since this is in effect a mini-course in biblical futurology.
3. Your particular view of the future may differ considerably from that presented by the authors. You may want to introduce what your church or denomination believes in the section on the future.
4. If you do not have enough background to feel at home in the sections on the future, you may want to get a book from your church library or Christian bookstore like *The Coming Russian Invasion of Israel* by Thomas McCall and Zola Levitt (Moody Press). Remember that the danger is not that you know too little, but that you want to share too much in such an abbreviated lesson.
5. Develop an outline of events from the material in the chapter. For clarity you may want to develop a horizontal line, with the events strung out along it.

Setting the Stage

Begin by asking: "What would happen if a majority of the people in the world lived by the laws of the kingdom we have been discussing during the past weeks?" The question is whether God would immediately bring on the Millennium. The events described in this chapter would indicate a steady march of history toward judgment because the laws of the kingdom will not appeal to the majority of any generation. That does not, however, change their validity for us and our children. And because they are so important, let's do a quick review of them.

Now use either a chalkboard or overhead transparency to list each law, drawing on the unique aspects of each to drive home the central ideas.

Wind up the discussion with the second and third paragraphs on page 212.

Looking Ahead

Long before Syrian gunners were manning Soviet SAM missiles prophetic teachers were pointing to chapters 38 and 39 of Ezekiel as a scenario that involved the Russians. Only recently, however, have such teachers found where the United States might possibly fit into the action-packed series of events. So read Ezekiel 38:1-7, 13. Have an overhead ready so you can present a total list of place names (or write them on the chalkboard as you read). Leave space to enter the suggested modern counterparts (pp. 213, 214).

Now ask questions like: "Who is in total control of the situation, according to verse 4?" You see, they think this confederacy warring against Israel is their idea, but it is God leading them to destruction as judgment for their godlessness. Let someone read Ezekiel 39:6-7, which reveals God's objective in all this.

If only Ezekiel told us about the upheaval of the end times, we might pass over it. But Revelation provides some dramatic specifics. Read Revelation 17:9-14 and ask: "What indications are there that we may be seeing this confederation taking shape today?" Then move on to Revelation 13:16-17 and ask: "What developments in technology make this a realistic possibility today?"

Can Jesus Be Far Behind?

While the high drama of international events holds the news spotlight, what is going on in heaven and among believers? Revelation 19 provides the answer. Have someone read verses 6-9 and ask:

"What is God preparing for the members of the invisible kingdom?" Move to verses 11 through 16 and ask: "What is Jesus Christ doing at this time?" Now notice how the description of Armageddon in verses 17–19 matches what Ezekiel predicted in chapter 38. The upshot of the battle is described in verse 20.

What happens next? Read Revelation 20:1–10 (the coming of the Millennium described by the authors on pages 216, 217). And who will rule? (See the top of p. 218 and 2 Tim. 2:12.)

What happens to Satan for the period the believers are ruling with Christ? (See Rev. 20:1–3.) Though Satan may be down, he is not out. (See vv. 7–9.)

Why does God let this happen? The explanation is in the parables of Matthew 13:24–43. What does this tell us about the removal of the evil ones?

What is the final step? (See 1 Cor. 15:22–28.)

Making It Happen

This is the thirteenth Sunday of study. What has happened in the lives of those in the group? Rather than belabor them with a lot of closing admonition, why not have one testimony for each law of the kingdom—a four to five sentence description that says, "I tried it. It works"? You will have to plan for the time. Or you could plan a social evening, a potluck, at which you share what God has done in your group as a result of implementing the laws of the kingdom. One person's testimony may trigger ideas in several others for ways to bring the invisible world into action in the visible world.

Another approach would be a commitment time, beginning with a call for those who have not yet accepted Christ as personal Savior to do so.

Another idea would be to read each law aloud and then allow for a period of twenty seconds of personal meditation and quiet commitment.

Let the Holy Spirit lead you in being creative. And wouldn't it be exciting to have an anniversary get-together a year later to rehearse what God has done through implementing the laws of the kingdom!

75